MANCHESTER UNITED
THE OFFICIAL ANNUAL 2016

Written by Steve Bartram and Gemma Thompson
Designed by Daniel James

A Grange Publication

©2015. Published by Grange Communications Ltd., Edinburgh, under licence from Manchester United Football Club. Printed in the EU.

ISBN 978-1-910199-50-3

INTRODUCTION - LOUIS VAN GAAL

Hello and welcome to the 2016 Manchester United Annual.

I must start by saying thank you to all the United supporters around the world for making me feel so welcome in my first year as the club's manager.

I thank you on behalf of my players and my staff as well, you've been amazing, especially for me. I felt the warmth of the fans from the first moment I took the job which is an experience I have not had at other clubs. Even when we had very disappointing results at the start of the 2014/15 season and had very few points, the fans were fantastic.

You, the supporters, have represented this huge club magnificently and you can rest assured that I, the players and the staff are all working hard to do the same. This club has a great history of success, and it is our collective intention to continue that tradition at Old Trafford.

My first season at the club was a step forward because we finished fourth and returned to European football. The aim always has to be to improve. None of us will be happy to finish in fourth position every year, so we must continue to get better. We have said farewell to some players and welcomed in new signings, and the squad is now much more balanced as we look to do well in all competitions in 2015/16.

Louis van Gaal

SEASON REVIEW 2014/15

AUGUST

A perfect pre-season campaign in the United States saw the Reds overcome a string of top European sides, including Real Madrid and Liverpool, and yielded the International Champions Cup. When preparations were rounded off by a last-gasp victory over Valencia at Old Trafford, hopes were high for the new campaign. Louis van Gaal's new-look side was forced to undergo a baptism of fire, however, with a home defeat to Swansea City followed by low-key Premier League draws against Sunderland and Burnley. The low point of the month, however, came in a heavy Capital One Cup defeat at League One's MK Dons, a result which preceded a huge overhaul by van Gaal as he moulded his squad.

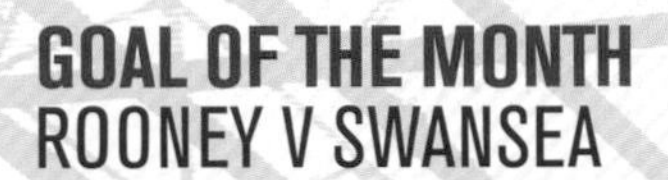

GOAL OF THE MONTH
ROONEY V SWANSEA

United's season got off to a nightmarish start against Garry Monk's impressive Swans, but the outstanding moment of a tough month came when skipper Wayne Rooney acrobatically equalised with a technically brilliant overhead kick from close range.

PLAYER OF THE MONTH
PHIL JONES

Despite having to acclimatise to a new formation with three central defenders, the England international shone as an experienced lynchpin in an injury-hit defence and displayed fine form throughout August.

SOUNDING OFF

"If you see the players that we have, we can play good football. It's just a matter of keeping working, believing and being patient."
Juan Mata

RESULTS

UNITED 1 SWANSEA 2
16 AUGUST - PREMIER LEAGUE

SUNDERLAND 1 UNITED 1
24 AUGUST - PREMIER LEAGUE

MK DONS 4 UNITED 0
26 AUGUST - CAPITAL ONE CUP

BURNLEY 0 UNITED 0
30 AUGUST - PREMIER LEAGUE

SEPTEMBER

A timely international break allowed van Gaal to substantially bolster his squad ahead of the Reds' next outing, with Radamel Falcao, Daley Blind and Marcos Rojo added to the roster. Inspired by goals from Angel Di Maria, Ander Herrera, Wayne Rooney and Juan Mata, a resounding win over Queens Park Rangers got the season belatedly off and running. An impressive first hour at Leicester City extended the feeling that United had turned a corner, until a stunning late fightback from the hosts inflicted a 3-5 defeat. Old Trafford would prove to be a sanctuary for much of the campaign, however, and goals from Wayne Rooney and Robin van Persie secured a narrow win over West Ham to end the month on a high note.

GOAL OF THE MONTH
DI MARIA V LEICESTER

Few players on the planet could have executed the Argentinian's impudent finish at the King Power Stadium. Gaining possession at top speed, Di Maria burst into the Leicester area and scooped an incredible finish over Kasper Schmeichel to prompt applause from even the home supporters.

PLAYER OF THE MONTH
ANGEL DI MARIA

The most expensive player in British football history quickly demonstrated his bottomless talent pool, notching goals against QPR and Leicester while thrilling with his every touch.

RESULTS

UNITED 4 QPR 0
14 SEPTEMBER – PREMIER LEAGUE

LEICESTER 5 UNITED 3
21 SEPTEMBER – PREMIER LEAGUE

UNITED 2 WEST HAM 1
27 SEPTEMBER – PREMIER LEAGUE

SOUNDING OFF

"Beating West Ham goes further than just three points. It was absolutely vital for everyone's belief and the fans' belief."
Robin van Persie

OCTOBER

The Reds strung together successive victories for the first time in 2014/15, beating Everton through goals from Angel Di Maria and Radamel Falcao, but the three points were owed in huge part to a sensational display from David De Gea, who made a string of invaluable stops to keep the Toffees at bay. Another international break served to stem United's flow, however, and it required goals from Marouane Fellaini and Daley Blind to secure a frustrating 2-2 draw at West Bromwich Albion. The month ended on another stalemate, but a 1-1 result against Jose Mourinho's Chelsea felt more like a victory after Robin van Persie thrashed home an injury-time equaliser at the Stretford End to send Old Trafford into delirium.

GOAL OF THE MONTH
FELLAINI V WEST BROM

Ater a frustrating first season at Old Trafford, the giant Belgian kickstarted his Reds career with a superb first goal for the club. Taking Di Maria's cross on his chest, Fellaini quickly shifted the ball before thundering a shot high into Boaz Myhill's goal.

PLAYER OF THE MONTH
DAVID DE GEA

The Spaniard was on top form all month, but put in an utterly sensational display against Everton in which he became the first Premier League goalkeeper to save a Leighton Baines penalty, then topped that with two staggering injury-time saves.

SOUNDING OFF

"The most pleasing thing is that we believe in making a goal even when the scoreline is bad. The players are running until the 90th minute to equalise or win."
Louis van Gaal

RESULTS

UNITED 2 EVERTON 1
5 OCTOBER - PREMIER LEAGUE

WEST BROM 2 UNITED 2
20 OCTOBER - PREMIER LEAGUE

UNITED 1 CHELSEA 1
26 OCTOBER - PREMIER LEAGUE

NOVEMBER

Despite opening the month with a narrow defeat at Manchester City, United's season began in earnest in November, with Juan Mata smashing home the only goal of a tight game against Crystal Palace to start a run of six successive Premier League victories. Next, the Reds travelled to Arsenal for a vital Saturday evening encounter and though David De Gea was again required to be on top form, the Reds staged a superb smash-and-grab victory through a Kieran Gibbs own-goal and Wayne Rooney's late clincher on the counter-attack. A comprehensive 3-0 win over Hull City rounded off the month in style, with Chris Smalling, Rooney and Robin van Persie all finding the target against Steve Bruce's Tigers.

GOAL OF THE MONTH
VAN PERSIE V HULL CITY

"I needed that," said the Dutchman, after his stunning strike against Hull City. Having struggled to find his best form in the early weeks of the season, van Persie demonstrated his class with a thunderous 25-yard effort to kill off the Tigers.

PLAYER OF THE MONTH
DAVID DE GEA

The Spaniard continued his fine run of form, keeping 10-man United in the Manchester derby for long periods and also repelling Arsenal's unrelenting attacks at the Emirates to further cement his status as one of the world's very best goalkeepers.

RESULTS

MANCHESTER CITY 1 UNITED 0
2 NOVEMBER – PREMIER LEAGUE

UNITED 1 CRYSTAL PALACE 0
8 NOVEMBER – PREMIER LEAGUE

ARSENAL 1 UNITED 2
22 NOVEMBER – PREMIER LEAGUE

UNITED 3 HULL CITY 0
29 NOVEMBER – PREMIER LEAGUE

SOUNDING OFF

"Our downfall this season is that we've had to change the team too much and we haven't had a consistent run with this squad. Hopefully that will change now."
Michael Carrick

DECEMBER

A typically packed festive fixture list required a little luck on occasion, particularly in December's early weeks, as United saw off heavy late pressure from Stoke to seal a 2-1 win through Marouane Fellaini and Juan Mata, then required a Robin van Persie brace to pinch three points at Southampton. The Dutchman also scored against Liverpool, as did Mata and Wayne Rooney, but it was goalkeeper David De Gea who stole the show in a brilliant virtuoso display, before Radamel Falcao's header secured a draw at Aston Villa. Newcastle were then brushed aside at Old Trafford, with Rooney's double followed by a van Persie header, but the year ended on a mixed note with a brilliant first-half display going unrewarded in a goalless draw at Spurs.

GOAL OF THE MONTH
ROONEY V LIVERPOOL

Just moments after De Gea's key save from Raheem Sterling, a swift counter-attack put United into an invaluable lead, with Antonio Valencia brilliantly creating space for Rooney's composed finish.

PLAYER OF THE MONTH
WAYNE ROONEY

The skipper's influence shone throughout the month, even though he was asked to moonlight in a relatively unfamiliar midfield role, and his haul of three goals in five games marked an impressive return too.

RESULTS

UNITED 2 STOKE 1
2 DECEMBER – PREMIER LEAGUE

SOUTHAMPTON 1 UNITED 2
8 DECEMBER – PREMIER LEAGUE

UNITED 3 LIVERPOOL 0
14 DECEMBER – PREMIER LEAGUE

ASTON VILLA 1 UNITED 1
20 DECEMBER – PREMIER LEAGUE

UNITED 3 NEWCASTLE 1
26 DECEMBER – PREMIER LEAGUE

TOTTENHAM 0 UNITED 0
28 DECEMBER – PREMIER LEAGUE

SOUNDING OFF

"It's a good end to the year with a good run of results. It has been a long time since we lost the last game so we have to keep going, and we have to keep playing great football."
Juan Mata

JANUARY

After ending 2014 on an impressive run of form, the hectic festive calendar appeared to take its toll on the Reds, who faced a series of physically challenging outings in the opening month of 2015. Radamel Falcao ensured a share of the spoils at Stoke City, while it took second-half goals from Ander Herrera and Angel Di Maria to navigate the plucky FA Cup challenge of Yeovil Town, before Southampton rode their luck at Old Trafford to nab a damaging 1-0 away win. Louis van Gaal's men bounced back in the Premier League with important victories over Queens Park Rangers (with goals from Marouane Fellaini and James Wilson) and Leicester City (Robin van Persie, Falcao and a Wes Morgan own-goal), but a goalless FA Cup draw at League Two's Cambridge United made for chastening viewing.

GOAL OF THE MONTH
HERRERA V YEOVIL TOWN

The Reds' FA Cup third round trip to Yeovil was following the giants vs plucky underdogs narrative perfectly, until substitute Ander Herrera thundered home an unstoppable 25-yard effort on the turn to spoil the story.

PLAYER OF THE MONTH
ANTONIO VALENCIA

The Ecuadorian spent much of the 2014/15 season moonlighting impressively in a defensive role, firstly as a wing-back but largely as a right-back, and his form was never better than during a strong start to the New Year.

RESULTS

STOKE 1 UNITED 1
1 JANUARY - PREMIER LEAGUE

YEOVIL TOWN 0 UNITED 2
4 JANUARY - FA CUP

UNITED 0 SOUTHAMPTON 1
11 JANUARY - PREMIER LEAGUE

QPR 0 UNITED 2
17 JANUARY - PREMIER LEAGUE

CAMBRIDGE 0 UNITED 0
23 JANUARY - FA CUP

UNITED 3 LEICESTER CITY 1
31 JANUARY - PREMIER LEAGUE

SOUNDING OFF

"It's quite tight. We must fight hard in the remaining games to finish as high as possible. It's a long season and we've picked ourselves up of late, so we need to keep the results coming for the fans."
Antonio Valencia

FEBRUARY

Progress in the FA Cup continued to add excitement to United's season, with Cambridge seen off in the fourth round replay thanks to goals from Juan Mata, Marcos Rojo and James Wilson, before Ander Herrera, Marouane Fellaini and a Wayne Rooney penalty secured a comeback victory at Preston North End in the fifth round. The Premier League, however, provided greater problems, with Daley Blind's last-gasp equaliser required to snatch a point at West Ham. Although Chris Smalling's brace and a Robin van Persie penalty saw off the spirited challenge of Burnley, a narrow defeat in a tight game at Swansea City all but ended the Reds' hopes of regaining the Premier League title. Skipper Wayne Rooney ensured the month ended on a high, however, with a decisive brace at home to Sunderland.

GOAL OF THE MONTH
HERRERA V SWANSEA

On a frustrating afternoon at the Liberty Stadium, the Reds' no.21 provided the outstanding moment of quality to put the visitors into a short-lived lead, drilling home from distance after a sublime passing move.

PLAYER OF THE MONTH
ANDER HERRERA

The Spaniard had found starts hard to come by in the early months of his United career, but thrived upon establishing himself in Louis van Gaal's plans and scored neat goals at Preston and Swansea.

RESULTS

UNITED 3 CAMBRIDGE 0
3 FEBRUARY – FA CUP 4TH ROUND REPLAY

WEST HAM 1 UNITED 1
8 FEBRUARY – PREMIER LEAGUE

UNITED 3 BURNLEY 1
11 FEBRUARY – PREMIER LEAGUE

PRESTON 1 UNITED 3
16 FEBRUARY – FA CUP 5TH ROUND

SWANSEA 2 UNITED 1
21 FEBRUARY – PREMIER LEAGUE

UNITED 2 SUNDERLAND 0
28 FEBRUARY – PREMIER LEAGUE

SOUNDING OFF

"Scoring goals and helping the team win is always my aim. When you score you get a mixture of feelings, depending on the game, what score it is and if it's a winning goal or a last-minute goal or the fourth in a 4-0 win, for example. It's always a great feeling to score and to see the joy you bring to so many people. It's a privilege to be able to do it."
Wayne Rooney

MARCH

Ashley Young's last-minute strike secured a smash-and-grab victory over Newcastle at St James' Park as the Reds continued to mount a charge for a top-four finish, and Champions League qualification became the season's sole remaining aim when Danny Welbeck returned to Old Trafford to fire Arsenal into the FA Cup semi-finals. The Reds' response, however, was emphatic, with the best performance of the season to date reserved for Tottenham's vital visit to Old Trafford. First-half goals from Marouane Fellaini, Michael Carrick and Wayne Rooney tied up the points for Louis van Gaal's side, who duly eclipsed that in their next game. On-song Liverpool were impressively overpowered at Anfield, where Juan Mata's spectacular brace secured an invaluable victory for the Reds.

GOAL OF THE MONTH
MATA V LIVERPOOL

Mata's opening goal was impressive enough, but his second provided perhaps the outstanding moment of the season, as he silenced Anfield with a stunning scissor kick to put the Reds two goals up.

PLAYER OF THE MONTH
JUAN MATA

The crafty Spanish playmaker shone in a midfield role throughout the month, and ensured himself of a permanent place in club folklore with a match-winning brace against Liverpool at Anfield.

RESULTS

NEWCASTLE 0 UNITED 1
4 MARCH – PREMIER LEAGUE

UNITED 1 ARSENAL 2
9 MARCH – FA CUP QUARTER-FINAL

UNITED 3 TOTTENHAM 0
15 MARCH – PREMIER LEAGUE

LIVERPOOL 1 UNITED 2
22 MARCH – PREMIER LEAGUE

SOUNDING OFF

"Anfield is the place to win, it's a massive game. It doesn't matter where we are in the league, or where they are, it is always special but it had that extra bit of importance."
Michael Carrick

APRIL

Having played their way into top form, United continued to impress as the season entered its penultimate month, and Tim Sherwood's revitalised Aston Villa side were gradually worn down by a pair of Ander Herrera strikes and Wayne Rooney's brilliant hooked volley. The performance of the season, however, was reserved for the Manchester derby, where Sergio Aguero's two goals merely provided the bookends in a tale of United dominance. Ashley Young equalised, before Marouane Fellaini, Juan Mata and Chris Smalling gave the Reds a thumping derby win – a first since December 2012 – and even sparked talk of a late title charge. A narrow defeat at champions-elect Chelsea put paid to those thoughts, while a limp reverse at Everton ensured a misleading end to a largely positive month.

GOAL OF THE MONTH
ROONEY V ASTON VILLA

An incredible show of dexterity and quick thinking from the skipper, who brilliantly controlled Angel Di Maria's cross with his left foot, then duly spun and hammered home a right-footed shot which gave Brad Guzan no chance.

PLAYER OF THE MONTH
ANDER HERRERA

Starting the month with a clinically-taken brace against Aston Villa, the Spaniard continued his splendid run of form with a series of dominant midfield displays, including a superb outing in the Manchester derby.

SOUNDING OFF

"We weren't ourselves in the first 15 minutes against City, but we dominated from there on and in the second half we really kicked on. You could sense even in the warm-up that the atmosphere was going to be special. We lost against City earlier in the season so it was massive to beat them and the fans really stuck with us."
Chris Smalling

RESULTS

UNITED 3 ASTON VILLA 1
4 APRIL – PREMIER LEAGUE

UNITED 4 MAN CITY 2
12 APRIL – PREMIER LEAGUE

CHELSEA 1 UNITED 0
18 APRIL – PREMIER LEAGUE

EVERTON 3 UNITED 0
26 APRIL – PREMIER LEAGUE

MAY

The return of long-serving midfielder Darren Fletcher prompted a warm outpouring of affection at the start of May, but that was the only positive to emerge from an afternoon on which Tony Pulis' West Brom side snatched a 1-0 victory to inflict the Reds' third successive defeat. That run came to an end after a gritty performance at Crystal Palace in which Marouane Fellaini headed home a late winner to confirm passage to the 2015/16 Champions League qualifiers. Any hopes of side-stepping that hurdle and making it straight into the group stages were dashed, however, as the season finished on a pair of draws: 1-1 at home to Arsenal and a goalless draw at Hull City which confirmed the Tigers' relegation.

GOAL OF THE MONTH
HERRERA V ARSENAL

The eighth and final goal of the Spaniard's debut season in England was a sublime effort. Ashley Young's fine wing-play culminated in a deep cross which fell perfectly for Herrera to guide home with a magnificently controlled volley.

PLAYER OF THE MONTH
ASHLEY YOUNG

The winger ended his best season as a United player in a fittingly strong fashion; providing three assists in four appearances, including two in the Reds' invaluable victory at Crystal Palace to arrest a run of three straight defeats.

RESULTS

UNITED 0 WEST BROM 1
2 MAY – PREMIER LEAGUE

CRYSTAL PALACE 1 UNITED 2
9 MAY – PREMIER LEAGUE

UNITED 1 ARSENAL 1
17 MAY – PREMIER LEAGUE

HULL 0 UNITED 0
24 MAY – PREMIER LEAGUE

SOUNDING OFF

"There are certainly signs of moving in the right direction and signs of big improvement. All in all, we can be satisfied with getting in the top four but it's not worth celebrating. Hopefully we can do a bit of celebrating next season."
Michael Carrick

SUMMER SIGNINGS

MEET THE MEN WHO ARRIVED AT UNITED IN THE SUMMER OF 2015...

SERGIO ROMERO

20

Born: 22 February 1987; Bernardo de Irigoyen, Argentina
Previous clubs: Racing Club, AZ Alkmaar, Sampdoria, Monaco (loan)
Joined United: 27 July 2015
International team: Argentina

Having gained invaluable experience on the grandest stages at club and international level, Sergio Romero brought big-game know-how to United's ranks following his transfer from Sampdoria. The Argentinian was part of the AZ Alkmaar team which stunned Dutch football under Louis van Gaal by winning the 2008/09 Eredivisie title, and being reunited with his former manager was an emotional experience for Sergio upon completing his move to the Reds. "It's perfect that I am back with my old manager. It makes me emotional," he said. "I owe Louis van Gaal so much. I will tell you what I told the boss the first time we worked together: that when you have an Argentine in your team, you get a never-give-up mentality." Having endured difficult spells at Sampdoria and Monaco, where he hardly played despite being an international regular, Romero is now vying for regular involvement at Old Trafford.

7

MEMPHIS

Born: 13 February 1994; Moordrecht, Netherlands
Previous club: PSV Eindhoven
Joined United: 12 June 2015
International team: Netherlands

Having taken the Dutch league by storm and topped the division's scoring charts at the age of just 21, Memphis arrived at Old Trafford with a bright future ahead of him. Blessed with pace, confidence and skill in abundance, the powerful forward brings menace to a variety of positions across United's attacking line, be it cutting in from the left flank or probing in support of a main striker. Although he arrived in England as an unknown to those without knowledge of Dutch football, Memphis was already well known to several figures at United, having worked with Albert Stuivenberg and Louis van Gaal during his rise through the Netherlands' international ranks. He was also a team-mate of Daley Blind, who was quick to vouch for the youngster's talents, saying: "He is a player who can change games. He's young, talented and wants to work hard. He always wants to better himself on the training pitch."

9

ANTHONY MARTIAL

Born: 5 December 1995; Massy, France
Previous clubs: Lyon, Monaco
Joined United: 1 September 2015
International team: France (Youth)

"I don't feel the pressure; I know there is pressure but I'm ready for it," was Anthony Martial's response to his deadline-day move to Old Trafford from AS Monaco. The highly-rated French youngster had created a stir in the youth ranks at Lyon and his shock move to Monaco came after just four senior appearances in French football. Armed with blistering pace and great physical presence, the forward was enlisted by United just hours before the 2015 summer transfer window closed and was quickly given a huge vote of confidence in the shape of the Reds' prestigious no.9 shirt. Upon completing the transfer, manager Louis van Gaal was quick to salute his new recruit, saying: "Anthony is a naturally talented, young, multi-functional forward with great potential. We have been watching him for a while now and he has developed immensely. He has all the attributes to become a top footballer." Though comparatively unknown upon his arrival in England, Anthony's transfer provided him with the platform to become a household name at United.

31

BASTIAN SCHWEINSTEIGER

Born: 1 August 1984; Kolbermoor, Germany
Previous club: Bayern Munich
Joined United: 14 July 2015
International team: Germany

Captain of the German national team and a world, European and Bundesliga champion with Bayern Munich, Bastian Schweinsteiger arrived at Old Trafford in July 2015 with an astonishing pedigree at both domestic and international level. The classy midfielder made his Bayern bow at 18 and notched 536 appearances and 22 major honours with the club during a 13-year stint in the German giants' first team. Upon completing his shock transfer to Old Trafford, Bastian admitted United were the only team he would have considered leaving his boyhood club for, and his capture certainly caused a stir in Louis van Gaal's squad. "He has had an incredible career so far," said fellow midfielder Michael Carrick, "and he is going to have a big say in this team and this squad going forward. He has been at the very top. He is a World Cup winner. What more can you ask for?"

28

MORGAN SCHNEIDERLIN

Born: 8 November 1989; Zellwiller, France
Previous clubs: Strasbourg, Southampton
Joined United: 14 July 2015
International team: France

Having repeatedly shone against United in Southampton's colours, Morgan Schneiderlin arrived at Old Trafford with supporters already well aware of his numerous attributes. The contribution of the all-action Frenchman had underpinned the Saints' rise from League One to the Premier League, and he evolved into one of the top flight's leading defensive midfielders during his six-year spell at St Mary's. An intelligent reader of the game, Morgan prowls menacingly in front of his defenders to offer sturdy protection to the backline, while also providing support in attack with his savvy passing and eye for goal. After choosing to join United over several alternative clubs in the summer of 2015, the French international was quick to appreciate the step up, saying: "To play here, it is not just about being a professional footballer. There is another dimension." With his boundless energy, Schneiderlin has undoubtedly also added a new dimension to Louis van Gaal's ranks.

36

MATTEO DARMIAN

Born: 2 December 1989; Legnano, Italy
Previous clubs: AC Milan, Padova (loan), Palermo, Torino
Joined United: 11 July 2015
International team: Italy

"He always looks solid and offers security," was the reaction of Reds legend Rio Ferdinand, when asked to summarise the contribution of Italian international Matteo Darmian. A product of AC Milan's youth system, the consistent, refined defender turned a loan spell to Torino permanent in 2013 and has since rapidly evolved ever since. Matteo's breakthrough on the international scene came at the 2014 World Cup in Brazil, and he has shone as his nation's starting right-back. Though he is two-footed enough to operate on either flank, Darmian started his Reds career as Louis van Gaal's preferred right-back and, after a spate of impressive early displays, looks set to pin down the position as his own for years to come.

2015/16 SQUAD LIST

GOALKEEPERS

1. DE GEA
20. S. ROMERO
50. JOHNSTONE

DEFENDERS

4. JONES
5. MARCOS ROJO
12. SMALLING
17. BLIND
23. SHAW
25. VALENCIA
33. MCNAIR
36. DARMIAN
42. BLACKETT

MIDFIELDERS

7. MEMPHIS
8. MATA
11. JANUZAJ
16. CARRICK
18. YOUNG
21. ANDER HERRERA
27. FELLAINI
28. SCHNEIDERLIN
31. SCHWEINSTEIGER
35. LINGARD
44. PEREIRA

FORWARDS

9. MARTIAL
10. ROONEY
19. WILSON

1

DAVID DE GEA

Born: 7 November 1990; Madrid, Spain
Previous club: Atletico Madrid
Joined United: 1 July 2011
United debut: 7 August 2011
vs Manchester City (N), Community Shield
International team: Spain

In a nutshell: Brimming with potential when he signed from Atletico Madrid in 2011, David has evolved into arguably the best young goalkeeper in the world, winning United's Player of the Year award for the last two seasons.

They say: "He's world-class and up there with the best goalkeepers in the game. He has the ability to produce saves at critical moments in a match even when he's not really had much to do. He's always alive to everything and has won us a lot of games." Phil Jones

50

SAM JOHNSTONE

Born: 25 March 1993; Preston
Previous clubs: Trainee, Oldham Athletic (loan), Scunthorpe United (loan), Walsall (loan), Yeovil (loan), Doncaster Rovers (loan)
Joined United: 1 July 2009
International team: England (youth)

In a nutshell: An FA Youth Cup-winner and repeated winner of silverware with the Reds' under-21s, Sam is an England youth international goalkeeper of promise and pedigree. His form during loan spells at Doncaster and Preston served only to reinforce the sense that Sam is destined for a successful career in the game.

They say: "Sam's had good experience out on loan and we've had great feedback on him. It's been a good test and a good challenge for him to get that experience, but he looks a commanding figure and he did really well." Warren Joyce

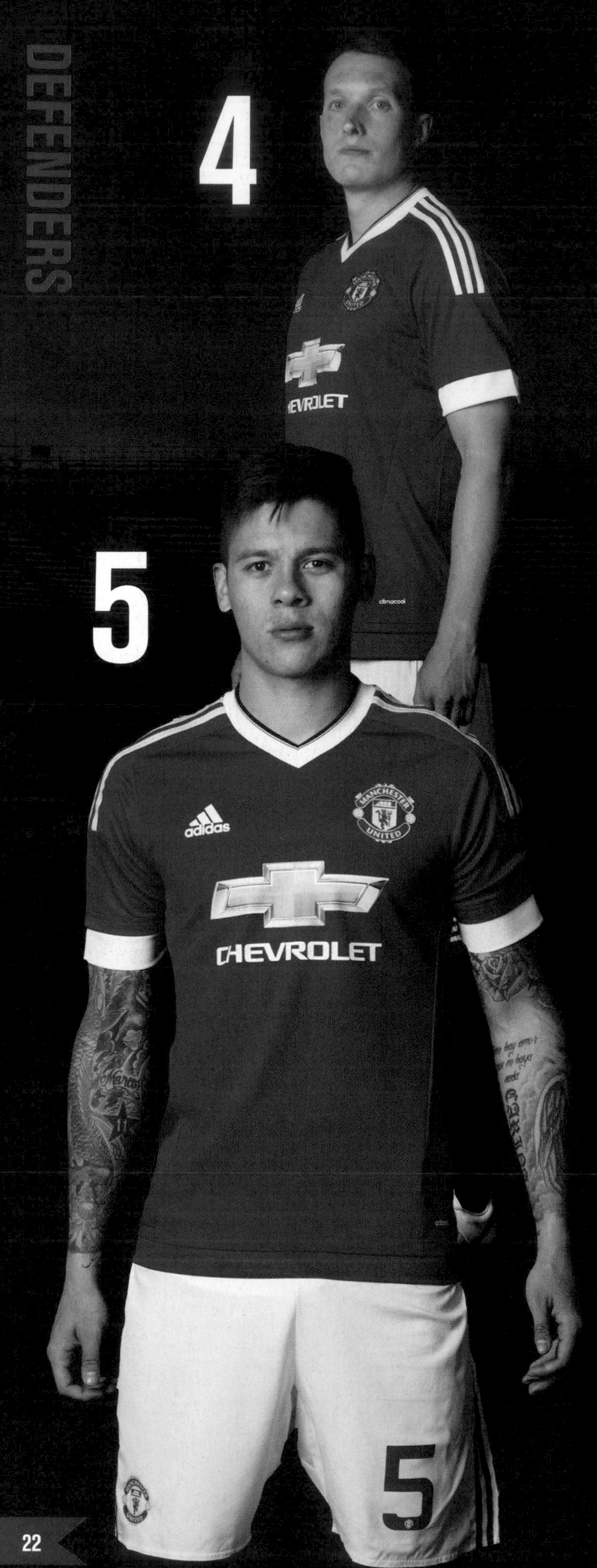

PHIL JONES

Born: 21 February 1992; Preston
Previous club: Blackburn Rovers
Joined United: 1 July 2011
United debut: 7 August 2011
vs Manchester City (N), Community Shield
International team: England

In a nutshell: Having demonstrated his ability to play at centre-back, full-back and in central midfield, the England international has settled in the first position and has made his full-blooded brand of defending an art-form since moving to Old Trafford.

They say: "His talent is unbelievable. His best position is centre-back but you could play him anywhere. I think you could play him centre forward. He's just that type of player. He's an animal for football. He grasps the game, he understands it."
Sir Alex Ferguson

MARCOS ROJO

Born: 20 March 1990; La Plata, Argentina
Previous clubs: Estudiantes, Spartak Moscow, Sporting Lisbon
Joined United: 20 August 2014
United debut: 14 September 2014
vs QPR (H), Premier League
International team: Argentina

In a nutshell: A robust, powerful left-sided defender who can operate in a variety of positions across the defence, Argentina international Rojo brings no-nonsense grit and graft to Louis van Gaal's backline.

They say: "Anyone who comes from Argentina is going to be a battler! Rojo is versatile – he can play centre-half, in a three or a four, left-back, left-wing back. He's a tough player and he got in the best XI at the World Cup, so it's good to have him here." Denis Irwin

12

CHRIS SMALLING

Born: 22 November 1989; Greenwich
Previous clubs: Maidstone United, Fulham
Joined United: 7 July 2010
United debut: 8 August 2010
vs Chelsea (N), Community Shield
International team: England

In a nutshell: Catapulted from non-league football to United's first team in the space of two years, Smalling arrived at Old Trafford full of untapped potential. In the ensuing half-decade, his displays have steadily grown in class and authority.

They say: "Everyone can see the improvement in Chris Smalling. His passing is a lot better, a lot crisper, his game has really come on. He can also carry the ball forward – Paul McGrath could do that and so could Gary Pallister – it's a great skill to have." Bryan Robson

17

DALEY BLIND

Born: 9 March 1990; Amsterdam, Netherlands
Previous clubs: Groningen (loan), Ajax
Joined United: 1 September 2014
United debut: 14 September 2014 vs QPR (H), Premier League
International team: Netherlands

In a nutshell: One of the most versatile players to have represented the Reds. Familiar to Louis van Gaal from their time together with the Dutch national team, Daley has been fielded in a variety of positions since arriving, demonstrating his class and intelligence in each role.

They say: "Daley has come in and helped to shore things up. He's very much a protective player, but he can pass the ball as well. He's looked strong and comfortable since he came to the club." Nicky Butt

23

LUKE SHAW

Born: 12 July 1995; Kingston-upon-Thames
Previous club: Southampton
Joined United: 27 June 2014
United debut: 27 September 2014 vs West Ham (H), Premier League
International team: England

In a nutshell: A product of Southampton's highly successful youth academy, the England international is one of the most exciting left-sided defenders around. After a steady debut term at United, he looks set to now unleash his unquestioned talent on a regular basis.

They say: "Luke can be anything he wants to be. He's incredible to watch sometimes. He's aggressive, good in the air, strong, quick, a good crosser, he can beat people, he can dribble... he's got it all." Gary Neville

ANTONIO VALENCIA

Born: 4 August 1985; Lago Agrio, Ecuador
Previous clubs: El Nacional, Villarreal, Wigan
Joined United: 30 June 2009
United debut: 9 August 2009
vs Chelsea (N), Community Shield
International team: Ecuador

In a nutshell: Signed to replace Cristiano Ronaldo on the right wing, Valencia provided an imposing presence and a string of assists in his early years as a Red. Recent seasons have included spells as a right-back and wing-back, demonstrating his diligence and versatility for the cause.

They say: "Antonio is a pure athlete – he is immense. It's the work he does that doesn't get noticed, things like carrying the ball up the pitch for 30 or 40 yards when you have been defending. If he can go down the line, then he is pretty hard to catch. He is a great team player and, when you are playing with him, you certainly appreciate that he is on your team." Michael Carrick

33

PADDY MCNAIR

Born: 27 April 1995; Ballyclare, Northern Ireland
Previous club: Ballyclare Colts
Joined United: 1 July 2011
United debut: 27 September 2014 vs West Ham (H), Premier League
International team: Northern Ireland

In a nutshell: A central midfielder turned defender, McNair entered Louis van Gaal's plans as an emergency stand-in at the start of the 2014/15 season, but his displays soon prompted full international recognition and a new long-term contract.

They say: "Paddy McNair has developed himself very well, not only as a central defender but at full-back. He has done it already in the second team [Under-21s] and has done it now at a higher level in the first team." Louis van Gaal

TYLER BLACKETT

Born: 2 April 1994, Manchester
Previous clubs: Blackpool (loan), Birmingham City (loan), Celtic (loan)
Joined United: 1 July 2002
United debut: 16 August 2014 vs Swansea (H), Premier League
International team: England (youth)

In a nutshell: A product of the Reds' youth system who featured in the 2011 FA Youth Cup success, Tyler is a local lad who operates at either left-back or in central defence. A hulking, powerful presence, his breakthrough in 2014/15 showcased his readiness for senior football.

They say: "Tyler is another young player that has risen through the Academy system to break into the first-team squad. He has great potential and I believe he is at the right club to continue his development and progression to become a great defender." Louis van Gaal

JUAN MATA

Born: 28 April 1988; Burgos, Spain
Previous clubs: Real Madrid (youth), Valencia, Chelsea
Joined United: 25 January 2014
United debut: 28 January 2014 vs Cardiff City (H), Premier League
International team: Spain

In a nutshell: A supremely gifted playmaker, Mata regularly shone against United in Chelsea's colours before his 2014 move to Old Trafford briefly broke the British transfer record. Ever since, supporters have been left in no doubt as to the Spaniard's brilliance.

They say: "He's just a little magician. So clever and with so much ability – he's a pleasure to watch. Playing against him over the years, I knew how good he was and we see it in training every day; some of the things he does really stand out. That left foot of his can open up any defence and, despite having such a slight physique, he's a terrific player."
Michael Carrick

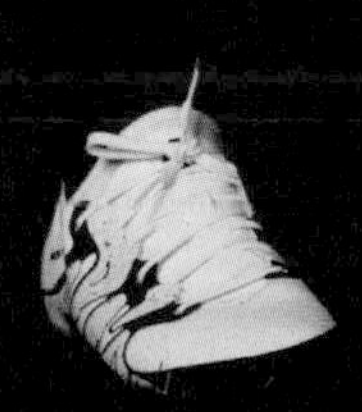

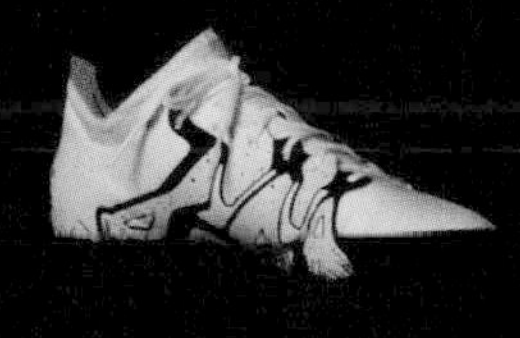

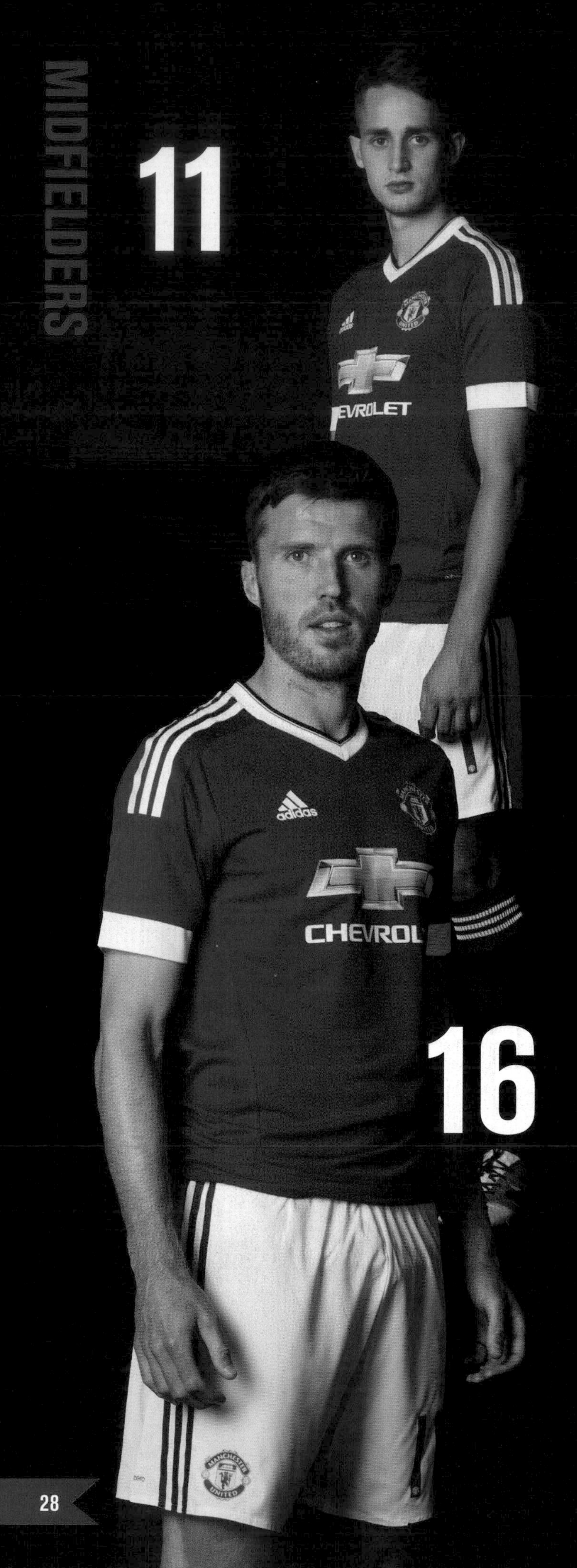

ADNAN JANUZAJ

Born: 5 February 1995; Brussels, Belgium
Previous clubs: Anderlecht, Borussia Dortmund (loan)
Joined United: 1 July 2011
United debut: 11 August 2013 vs Wigan (N), Community Shield
International team: Belgium

In a nutshell: The number of countries clamouring for Januzaj's services on the international stage demonstrated the scale of his talent. Belgium eventually claimed his services, and the classy playmaker is expected to become a top talent for club and country.

They say: "I think it's lovely to see how great Adnan has done over the last couple of years. He gives hope to the whole United spirit, a young lad coming through from the academy into the first team." Anders Lindegaard

MICHAEL CARRICK

Born: 29 July 1981; Wallsend
Previous clubs: West Ham, Swindon (loan), Birmingham (loan), Tottenham Hotspur
Joined United: 31 July 2006
United debut: 23 August 2006 vs Charlton Athletic (A), Premier League
International team: England

In a nutshell: The man at the United switchboard for so long since his 2006 arrival from Tottenham. A midfielder of supreme intellect and vision, Carrick dictates United's tempo and has played a major role in all the club's successes during his time in Manchester.

They say: "He is a player that can change a team. He always keeps the ball safe and tries to plays it forward. He gives stability to the team, he has great experience and is a great guy. It's amazing to play with him."
Juan Mata

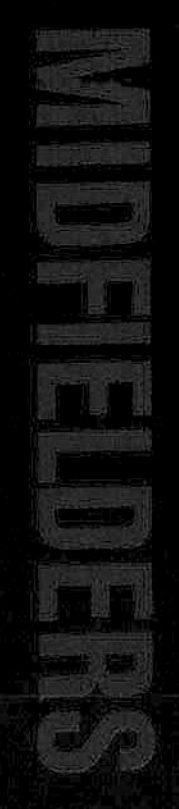

Born: 9 July 1985; Stevenage
Previous clubs: Watford, Aston Villa
Joined United: 1 July 2011
United debut: 7 August 2011
vs Manchester City (N), Community Shield
International team: England

In a nutshell: A versatile, diligent presence on either flank, Ashley enjoyed a steady opening to his Reds career after joining from Aston Villa. The arrival of Louis van Gaal invigorated his game, however, and he was one of the star performers during the 2014/15 campaign.

They say: "He is a player who wants to perform what you say. I think he fits well in my profile. He has quality but he always wants to improve and he can play in different positions. We have played also with wing-backs and I think that is his best position. But I can use him as a winger as well and he does a very good job."
Louis van Gaal

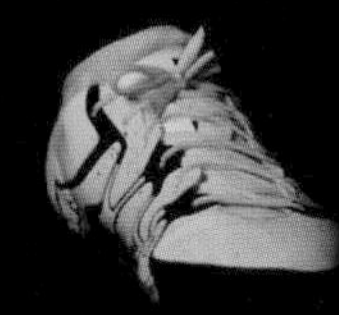

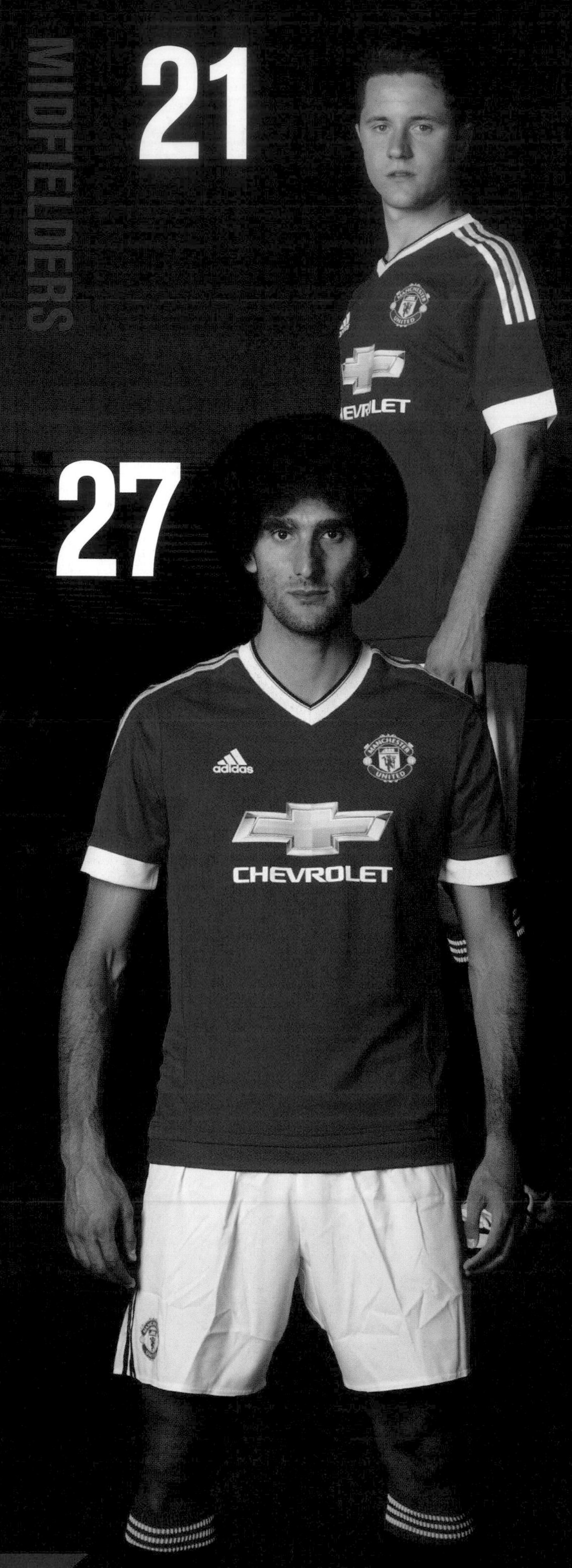

21 ANDER HERRERA

Born: 14 August 1989; Bilbao, Spain
Previous clubs: Real Zaragoza, Athletic Club
Joined United: 26 June 2014
United debut: 16 August 2014
vs Swansea (H), Premier League
International team: Spain (youth)

In a nutshell: An energetic midfielder who joined the Reds at the start of the 2014/15 campaign, Ander quickly established himself as a fans' favourite with his all-action approach, love of tackling and eye for spectacular and important goals.

They say: "He's crazy about football. He's always speaking about football and wants to know everything – he knows virtually every player in every league. We understand football and life in the same way – I think that's why we work so well together."
Juan Mata

27 MAROUANE FELLAINI

Born: 22 November 1987; Etterbeek, Belgium
Previous clubs: Standard Liege, Everton
Joined United: 2 September 2013
United debut: 14 September 2013
vs Crystal Palace (H), Premier League
International team: Belgium

In a nutshell: Another player who repeatedly shone in action against United, hulking Belgian international Fellaini joined from Everton in 2013. A tough, physically imposing presence who can play in midfield or further forward as a target man, occupying either role to often devastating effect.

They say: "He is a handful for defenders to mark. We like to play out from the back and if teams are pressing us then we have him as an option. He is probably the best in world football at bringing the ball down and getting us out of pressure and further up the pitch." Wayne Rooney

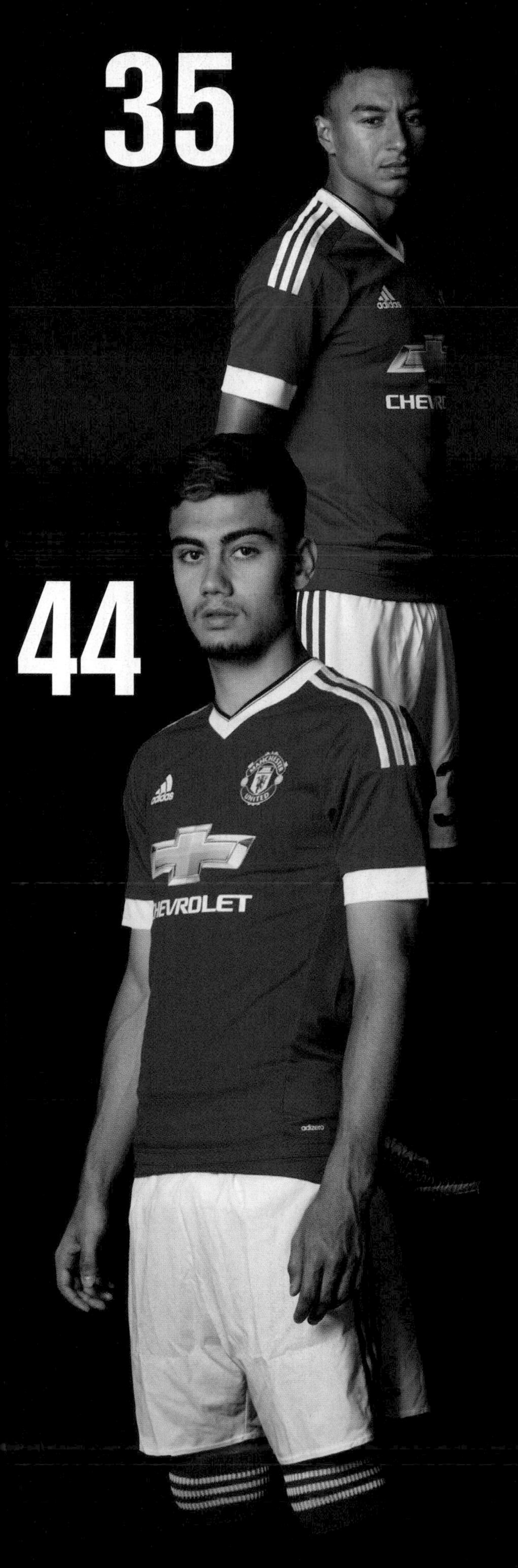

JESSE LINGARD

Born: 15 December 1992; Warrington
Previous clubs: : Leicester City (loan), Birmingham City (loan),Brighton & Hove Albion (loan), Derby County (loan)
Joined United: 1 July 2009
United debut: 16 August 2014 vs Swansea (H), Premier League
International team: England (youth)

In a nutshell: A sublimely sharp young playmaker, Jesse belied his small stature to make a big impact in the Reds' youth ranks. His crisp passing, intelligence and vision mark him out as a top prospect, and his success in various loan spells have confirmed his remarkable talent.

They say: "He's an intelligent footballer. He's got very clean feet, is sharp coming in from the line and has good movement. He's also got a goal in him because he's a calm finisher."
Gareth Southgate

ANDREAS PEREIRA

Born: 1 January 1996; Duffel, Belgium
Previous clubs: Lommel United, PSV Eindhoven
Joined United: 1 July 2012
United debut: 26 August 2014 vs MK Dons (A), League Cup
International team: Brazil (youth)

In a nutshell: One of the hottest young talents around. The Belgian-born Brazilian youth international is a classy, refined playmaker whose brimming talents look set to overspill into the Reds' first-team setup after he penned a new contract in the summer of 2015.

They say: "Andreas has all the attributes to become an integral part of the first team; great natural talent coupled with a good appetite to learn. I am pleased with his progression so far and look forward to working with him to develop his talent even further." Louis van Gaal

10

WAYNE ROONEY

Born: 24 October 1985; Liverpool
Previous club: Everton
Joined United: 31 August 2004
United debut: 28 September 2004 vs Fenerbahce (H), Champions League
International team: England

In a nutshell: United's talisman and leader. After arriving at Old Trafford with the potential to become the best English player in a generation, Rooney has enjoyed a long, silverware-laden Reds career. He is now team captain and is on course to become the club's all-time leading goalscorer.

They say: "Wayne is our leader. He is maybe the strongest guy - not only physically, but also mentally. I think we in the squad are following him always. He is our captain, our leader and our [biggest] character. I think he shows very, very well what Manchester United is."
Ander Herrera

19

JAMES WILSON

Born: 1 December 1995; Biddulph
Previous club: Trainee
Joined United: 1 July 2012
United debut: 6 May 2014
vs Hull City (H), Premier League
International team: England (youth)

In a nutshell: Blessed with pace, intelligence and a ruthless streak in front of goal, Wilson is one of the most exciting young strikers to emerge from the Reds' youth ranks in the Premier League era.

They say: "He's very direct, scores goals, has good pace and that added bonus of being a left-footer – they always tend to catch defenders off guard and it always looks more special when the left-footed strike goes in. I like his attitude, he looks a good player, a good prospect and one that everyone needs to keep an eye on." Teddy Sheringham

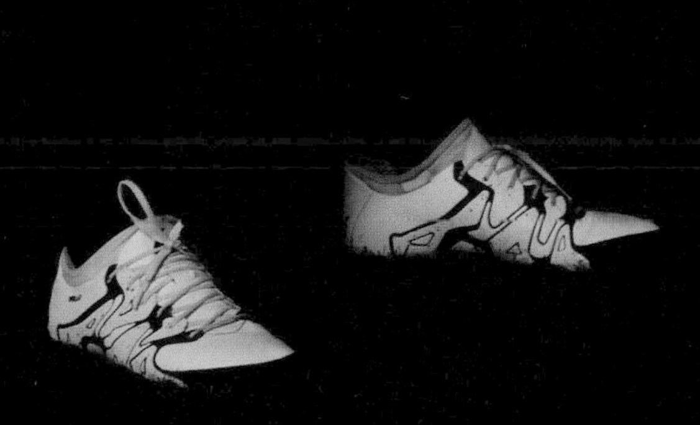

TRAINING TRADE SECRETS

Want to know who is the fastest United star in the squad, the most competitive in training and which Reds would make up the best five-a-side team? Here, the players reveal all about their team-mates and life at the Aon Training Complex...

WHAT'S THE BEST GOAL YOU'VE SEEN – OR SCORED – IN TRAINING?

"It was a goal I scored after we were knocking the ball about outside the area. The ball came to me and I didn't let it drop – I hit it first time. I liked that goal, it was a good one!"

ANTONIO VALENCIA

WHO IS MOST LIKELY TO SCORE A PICTURE-BOOK GOAL IN TRAINING?

"It would probably be Wayne [Rooney], with a volley or something. The ball will drop out to him and he'll just go for it when nobody else would think to do it and it'll fly into the top corner."

JAMES WILSON

DO YOU DO ANY SPECIFIC WORK IN THE GYM AS PART OF YOUR TRAINING REGIME?

"Yes, I do a lot of work in the gym. I am trying to be faster and stronger so I can be tougher when I go out on the pitch. I am doing a lot of short, sharp stuff so, when I turn a defender or go past a player, I can just get a few metres away from them with my acceleration."

ADNAN JANUZAJ

WHAT IS YOUR FAVOURITE PART OF TRAINING?

"My favourite part is when we play games, that's when the players really enjoy it. There is a lot of tactical training with the shape and the play. You enjoy that and it's great for you and your knowledge of the game."

WAYNE ROONEY

HOW SERIOUSLY DO YOU TREAT THE MATCHES YOU PLAY IN TRAINING?

"It's serious – you don't want to lose. I think that's built in us, whatever we play, whether it's table tennis on tour or a game of pool, snooker, anything... it's always competitive. When you get out on the training pitch, you don't want to go back inside the changing room and be on the end of some stick after the session! You always want to win."

MICHAEL CARRICK

WHICH FOUR COLLEAGUES WOULD YOU PICK TO JOIN YOU ON A FIVE-A-SIDE TEAM IF YOU WERE ABOUT TO START A MATCH NOW?

"I need a defender in there... I'll put Daley back there. Can I do a bench as well?! [Laughs]. Carras, Wazza and Juan."

ASHLEY YOUNG

WHICH PART OF TRAINING DO YOU ENJOY THE MOST?

"I'd probably say the games when we do 11 vs 11. At times it's fun to do small games and, more often than not, I enjoy them the most but I like to play 11 vs 11 as that gets you into the game mode rather than it just being training. It's very close to what you'll face at the weekend."

CHRIS SMALLING

WHO'S THE MOST COMPETITIVE IN TRAINING?

"Everybody is really competitive, that's what makes our sessions good. Wayne Rooney is really competitive! I like that spirit of winning – it inspires everyone and it's great to see that."

DALEY BLIND

MICHAEL'S MAGIC MOMENTS

In the summer of 2016, vice-captain Michael Carrick will celebrate 10 years as a Red. The midfielder made the move to Old Trafford in the summer of 2006 from Tottenham Hotspur and since then has gone on to win almost every honour in the English game. Here, our no.16 takes a special look back at16 different photographs from his United career so far, recalling some of the stand-out moments and reflecting on memorable days gone by...

BECOMING A RED

This was a very special day for me and my family. I'll always be very grateful for what both West Ham and Tottenham did for me, but to sign for United is something not many players get the chance to do. It's a club like no other and one I'm very proud to be part of.

MY DEBUT

I'd got an ankle injury during pre-season so I had to wait a little bit of time for my first game, but I came on as sub at Charlton and it was a great feeling to pull on that shirt for the first time.

STEPPING UP

Training can be quite daunting when you come into the club as a new player because you've got to earn the respect and the trust of your team-mates and prove to them you're good enough to be there. You have to give your all in every session.

MY FIRST UNITED GOAL

I think you feel relief more than anything to get your first goal on the board. It was quite a bit into the season by this point so I was pleased to get it and pleased with the finish in the win over Villa.

2007

SHEASY SHOCKS ANFIELD

I'd not seen that photo until recently. If I was to think of a specific memory from my time here this would be very near the top of my list. It was my first game at Anfield for United, we were going for the league, Scholesy got sent off and then Sheasy nicked a winner in the last minute... it's one of the highlights of my career so far.

SEVENTH HEAVEN

That was a night when everything just came together, beating Roma 7-1. It will probably go down as one of the great European nights at Old Trafford and for me to get two of the seven goals was a bit unusual and also very special!

2007

2007

JUST CHAMPION

To get my hands on the trophy for the first time was an unbelievable feeling. And once you experience that feeling, you want to do it again and again and again; that's always our aim at the start of every season.

2007

HAVING A LAUGH

This photo sums up the spirit at the club; it's been great the whole time I've been here. We have and have had some big players at United, but off the pitch we all get on very well and the banter in the dressing room is always fantastic.

MICHAEL'S MAGIC MOMENTS

A HAMMER BLOW

I remember Nani got sent off and it was a game against West Ham which we had to win. It was nice to score against my old team, but on the day it was all about us winning and I was pleased I could help us do that.

MAYHEM IN MOSCOW

I've got this photo up in my house and I honestly can't describe the feeling I had at this moment in time. If I could sum it up in three words I'd say, nervous, excited, giddy. It's the best feeling I've ever had as an instant feeling, and I don't think anything will ever match that minute or so after Edwin's save won us the Champions League.

BEST ON THE PLANET

As an achievement, winning the Club World Cup probably didn't get enough coverage or appreciation, but for us as players it was a massive achievement because you only get a chance to win it after winning the Champions League. It's just as big as the other trophies we've won and to be a world champion was a great feeling.

WEMBLEY WOE

That Barcelona team was probably the best team, not just that I've played against in my career so far, but the best I've ever seen play. On the night, in the 2011 Champions League final, we were in the game for a little bit, but we couldn't pull it off against a team who were simply at their peak.

2012

AN ANFIELD MILESTONE

I didn't know on the day that it was a milestone game for me – my 350th league appearance – but any win at Liverpool is one you always savour. Victories against them are something you never forget.

PLAYER OF THE SEASON

I can't put into words the influence that Sir Alex had on me and my career. He did so much for all of us as players and the confidence he'd give you was incredible. To win the Players' Player of the Season award, in Sir Alex's last year, meant an awful lot to me.

2013

2013

CONDUCTING THE CROWD

That was a very special day, parading the Premier League trophy through Manchester. Winning the title back after what had happened the year before and then having Scholesy and Sir Alex both retiring meant there were a lot of emotions. The reception we received as we drove through the city on the bus was absolutely sensational.

2015

TAKING CHARGE

Me and Wayne have been here a long time now so I suppose it was the natural thing in terms of the captaincy and vice-captaincy. It's something we're both proud of and all of us are enjoying working under the manager, and hopefully together we can bring the fans some success over the next few seasons.

JUAN MATA
MY MANCHESTER

As entrances go, Juan Mata's arrival at Manchester United was something pretty unique. No other player in the club's history has touched down in a helicopter to sign a contract with the Reds, but the Spanish playmaker is not your average footballer. While many spend their spare time relaxing, Mata prefers to explore Manchester, finding out more about the local culture and landmarks. "I am a curious person," he insisted after reflecting on a visit to an art gallery in the city centre followed by a walk up to the Northern Quarter, which offers an alternative take on Manchester culture.

Juan is also someone who was extremely keen to learn about the club's rich history soon after he joined in January 2014 and took time out to take a tour of the Old Trafford museum. The attacker writes a weekly blog about his career on and off the pitch and is also a real advocate of communicating with fans via social media. Here, we take a closer look at Mata's thoughts and feelings on life in Manchester and as a Red...

JUAN ON...

THE MAGIC OF UNITED

"From the outside you can see how big the club is, but it's only when you're inside and you come to somewhere like the museum that you really realise how big it is. It was really important for me to visit the museum – I wanted to know more about the history of the club, the trophies United have won and all the players who have played here. I even had a special tour with Paddy Crerand, who won the European Cup here in 1968. I think every player who arrives at a new club should know about the history of the club and what it means to play here."

JUAN ON...

FIRST GAME FEELINGS

"My debut is an experience I will never forget. It was just two or three days after I arrived [in January 2014] and everything went very quickly. The first time I went out onto the pitch was amazing, I remember the fans were singing my name. We won after a difficult run of results, the atmosphere was great and my team-mates were great with me; they have been since the first day. That night is something that will always be very high on my list of the best football experiences I've had. As a kid, I always wanted to be a professional footballer but I never thought I would have the career I'm having and play for the clubs I have played for. To have the chance to play for Manchester United is something I was never expecting. I am so happy to be here."

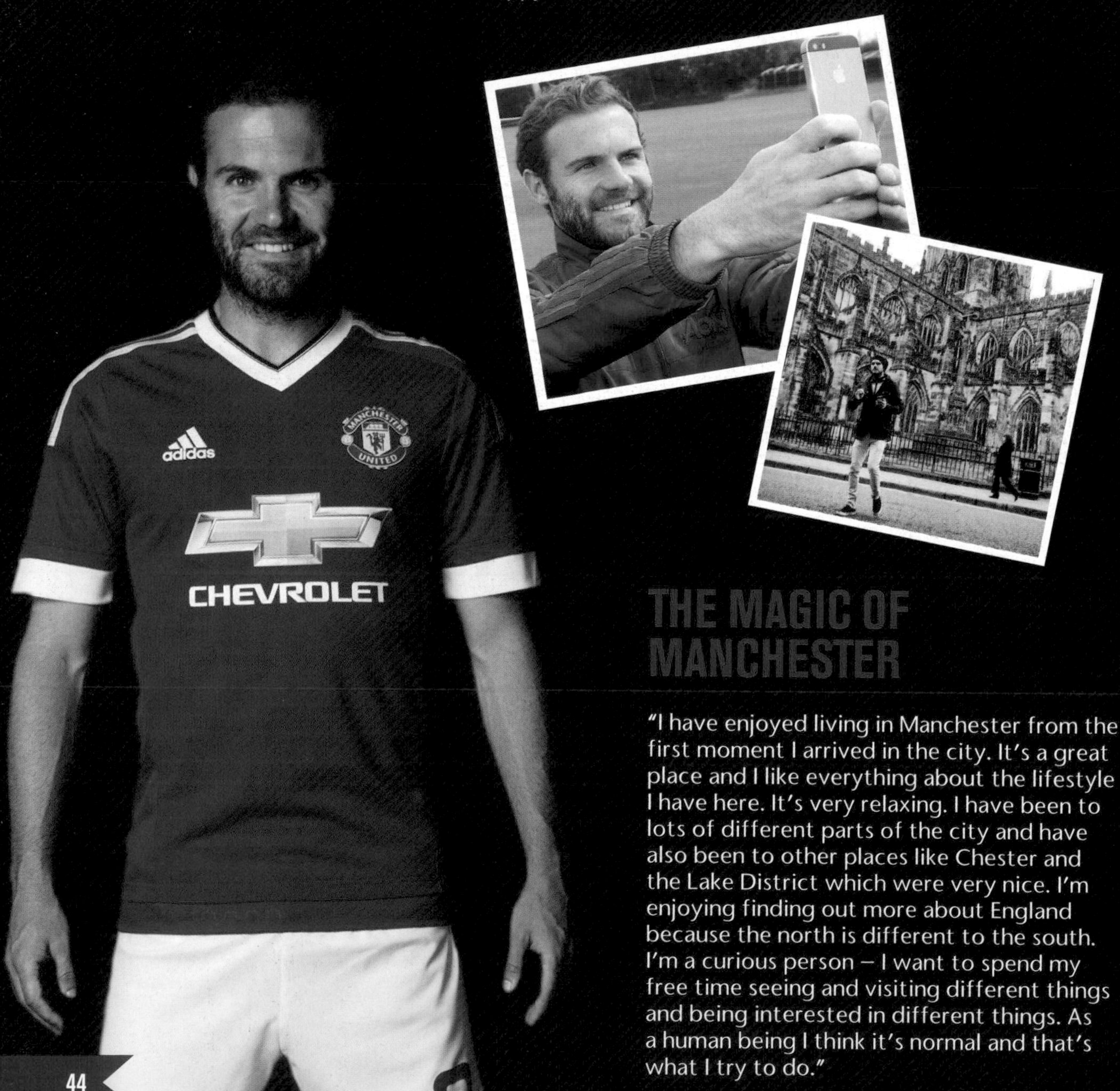

THE MAGIC OF MANCHESTER

"I have enjoyed living in Manchester from the first moment I arrived in the city. It's a great place and I like everything about the lifestyle I have here. It's very relaxing. I have been to lots of different parts of the city and have also been to other places like Chester and the Lake District which were very nice. I'm enjoying finding out more about England because the north is different to the south. I'm a curious person – I want to spend my free time seeing and visiting different things and being interested in different things. As a human being I think it's normal and that's what I try to do."

RED RELATIONSHIPS

"I am lucky to be part of a team with fantastic spirit. Everyone gets on well and I am particularly close to Ander [Herrera]. We have had a big Spanish contingent here over the last year or so with players like David [De Gea], Antonio [Valencia], Marcos [Rojo] and also [Radamel] Falcao and Angel [Di Maria]. Ander and I especially have a good understanding on the pitch too. I think it's because of the relationship we've had over the years and because we understand football and life in more or less the same way. Sometimes without speaking or looking we know where we're going to pass or where we're going to move on the pitch. Away from the pitch, we also watch a lot of football together too, although he does more than me – he forces me sometimes! He's crazy about football. He's always speaking about football and wants to know everything – he knows virtually every player in every league!"

THE BLOG

"I obviously enjoy writing it more when we win and have a good game! It's easier to do it then because you are feeling in a better mood.
I like to write the blog because it's a way for me to explain how I felt in a game, how things in Spanish football are going and explain about the other important things in my life such as what places I've visited, what music I like or movies or whatever. I think it's good because I get feedback from fans; they reply and leave me comments on social media and on the blog. It's something I really enjoy doing."

THE FANS

"There are so many things that I love about our fans. First of all the support they give to us at Old Trafford is amazing. When you play abroad on pre-season tours we see the millions of supporters we have around the world, and then when we play away in the league it's crazy how many people travel to watch us, and no matter if we win or lose they are always behind us. Their support is something you can't really explain with words."

STATESIDE STARS

WE LOOK BACK ON ANOTHER SUCCESSFUL TOUR TO THE UNITED STATES AND HEAR FROM CAPTAIN WAYNE ROONEY, SUMMER ARRIVAL MORGAN SCHNEIDERLIN AND YOUNG STRIKER JAMES WILSON ABOUT LIFE ON THE ROAD WITH THE REDS...

Louis van Gaal and his squad once again embarked on a summer tour to the United States in July 2015 as preparations continued in earnest for the 2015/16 season. The trip was the Reds' sixth pre-season visit across the pond since the turn of the century and came some 65 years after the club's first-ever trip there, back in 1950 for a close-season tour which included an incredible 12 matches!

Football, or soccer as it is more commonly known in the States, is a sport that's growing all the time in America, as is the support for United. The 2014 tour resulted in the Reds setting an attendance record for a soccer match in the country, with over 109,000 fans packed inside Michigan Stadium for the meeting with Real Madrid. And almost 200,000 supporters cheered on van Gaal's men during the four-game tour in 2015.

United legend David Beckham's time at LA Galaxy has played a big part in raising the profile of the game and Beckham's former team-mate and United's current assistant manager Ryan Giggs has been witness to the sizeable increase in interest from when he went over with the team in 2003 as a player to the most recent tour, and he believes it will only get bigger.

"The passion of the fans in the States has grown a lot. I was fortunate to go there more than 10 years ago and the support we've got has definitely increased. It was great back then but it's even bigger now," he explained. "You used to be able to walk out of your hotel and not get bothered, but now you walk out of the hotel and there are hundreds of fans there all day wanting a picture or an autograph or to catch a glimpse of the players, which is great. It's brilliant to see the support growing all the time for United in the States."

Tour 2015, presented by Aon, yielded a number of positive results and provided the perfect environment for the players to get ready for the 2015/16 campaign.

RESULTS

17 JULY: UNITED 1 CLUB AMERICA 0
SCHNEIDERLIN

INTERNATIONAL CHAMPIONS CUP
CENTURYLINK FIELD, SEATTLE.
ATTENDANCE: 46,857

Morgan Schneiderlin enjoyed a dream debut for the Reds as his early goal secured an opening tour win in Seattle.

21 JULY: UNITED 3 SAN JOSE EARTHQUAKES 1
MATA, MEMPHIS, PEREIRA

INTERNATIONAL CHAMPIONS CUP
AVAYA STADIUM, SAN JOSE.
ATTENDANCE: 18,000

Reds make it two wins from two as Memphis Depay nets his maiden United goal and Andreas Pereira heads home his first senior strike, in San Jose.

THE CAPTAIN

WAYNE ROONEY GIVES HIS REFLECTIONS ON THE TOUR AND REVEALS HIS EXCITEMENT AT UNITED'S SUMMER SIGNINGS...

"We had a really good pre-season. There were some tough games on tour, against Barcelona and PSG especially, but that's what you want. Pre-season is always about building your fitness up and if you get some tough games it's even better because it tests you even more mentally and physically.

America is always a great country to visit and the facilities were fantastic – we were looked after really well and were very grateful for that. The tour was great for the new players and helping them to settle in. Their arrival lifted everyone and I think it's an exciting time for the team. The new lads are quality players and we feel they can give us an extra gear to what we had last season. Obviously the players who have been here since last season understand how the manager wants us to work. For the first couple of months it was probably a bit difficult to take everything in and go out and perform last year, but we fully understand what he wants and it's great we've added even more quality to the squad.

I played up front with Memphis for part of the tour games and he's a fantastic talent. We're still working on things in training to try to get better together and get a better understanding of each other's games, which is important. It's gone well so far and I'm sure in the near future it'll get even better and there will be a lot of excitement around the strikers. We're all ready to play the games when the manager wants us.

I was pleased to score against Barcelona and it was very satisfying to get the win against them, particularly given the way we played. A lot of the younger players came on for the last 30 minutes and did really well against a quality team and that will give them a lot of confidence.

The games are obviously important in pre-season but as I said before the most important thing is building your fitness up and learning how the manager wants us to play from the start of the season. You always want to win the matches but our focus was always on being ready for the first game of the campaign. And now with the new players that have come in I feel we have the right squad to help us have a successful season."

25 JULY: UNITED 3
BARCELONA 1
ROONEY, LINGARD, JANUZAJ

INTERNATIONAL CHAMPIONS CUP
LEVI'S STADIUM, SANTA CLARA.
ATTENDANCE: 68,416

Van Gaal's men survive early scares to seal an impressive victory over the European champions as squad's youngsters shine in Santa Clara.

29 JULY: UNITED 0
PARIS SAINT-GERMAIN 2

INTERNATIONAL CHAMPIONS CUP, SOLDIER FIELD, CHICAGO.
ATTENDANCE: 61,351

Tour 2015 ends in disappointment as Zlatan Ibrahimovic inspires the French champions to victory in Chicago.

THE YOUNGSTER

JAMES WILSON LOOKS BACK ON HIS FIRST PRE-SEASON TRIP WITH THE SENIOR TEAM AND DISCUSSES HIS HOPES FOR THE FUTURE...

"Going on tour with the first team was an amazing experience and something I learnt a lot from. I had been training and involved with the squad for quite a bit of time before we went on tour and that definitely helped me, but the experience was even better than I thought it would be, mainly because you're together most of the time so it's a great opportunity to get to know everyone even more.

It was nice to get to know the new players as well. They're all really nice guys and I think it all felt very normal to them very early on, as everyone in the squad is always good at making new players feel at home.

There were a few young lads on the trip too who I know well so we spent quite a bit of time together off the pitch. A few of us came on together in the second half in the win over Barcelona which was a great game to be involved in. We just went out there and tried to do what the manager wanted us to do. Growing up with lads like Andreas [Pereira], Paddy [McNair], Jesse [Lingard] and Tyler [Blackett] and playing together a lot means we have a good relationship and are on the same wavelength. But I think everyone is like that in the squad because we are training with each other every day.

Like me, Sean Goss was experiencing his first tour and he enjoyed it as much as I did. He did well at the end of last year when he came up and trained with the first team. He has just gone from strength to strength and the tour can only help both of us to progress.

I feel like it's going to be an important season for me so I wanted to do my best on tour. I feel fit and I am just hoping not to get injured like last season. A couple of our strikers left the club in the summer so I hope I can get my chance. But to do that I know I need to show the manager my qualities out on the pitch and prove to him I can score goals for the first team. That's my aim and, after a really enjoyable pre-season tour, that's what I'll be working hard to do."

THE DEBUTANT

MORGAN SCHNEIDERLIN'S TRANSFER TO UNITED WAS CONFIRMED ON THE MORNING THE TEAM FLEW OUT TO THE STATES. HERE, THE FRENCHMAN RECALLS THE WHIRLWIND START TO HIS REDS CAREER…

"Signing for the club really is a dream come true for me and something I've been working towards throughout my career so far. Completing my move and going straight on tour was a really good thing because it meant I could spend virtually every hour of the day with the other players and get to know everyone better. There is no better way to adapt to a new club than spending every day with your team-mates. Everyone made me feel welcome from the first minute and I speak good English too, so that made things easier as well.

We received incredible support when we were in America but it wasn't something that surprised me. I've always been very aware of how big the club is and what it asks of the players. People around the world love Manchester United and the atmosphere around the club is crazy, but I knew it would be like that before I came. It was definitely a slightly different pre-season tour to what I've been used to. At Southampton we went to quiet places like Austria where some people recognised us but it was the complete opposite with United!

I must say my time at Southampton was the best learning curve for me. I met some great people there who helped me to progress and helped me realise how important it is to train every day and to work hard and that has prepared me in the best way possible for life at United. I felt ready when I joined and this season it's time for me to show it.

We did some great work on the training pitch on tour. Every manager has their different style of how they want to train and the gaffer here always likes us to have the ball. He is strict but that's because he wants us to be the best we can every time we train and be clever in what we do. You can only improve by training like that so I'm very happy to be involved and to learn.

It's a joy to train with the great players we have here. Training with the likes of Bastian Schweinsteiger and Michael Carrick week in and week out can only help you improve your game. The competition in midfield is intense but that competition is good for the team. At a club like United you would expect nothing else. Hopefully we can all play our part in making it a memorable season."

RED REWIND: THE 1995/96 DOUBLE

THE 2015/16 CAMPAIGN MARKS THE 20TH ANNIVERSARY OF ONE OF THE MOST FAMOUS SEASONS IN UNITED'S HISTORY: THE 1995/96 DOUBLE TRIUMPH.

Inspired by the returning genius of Eric Cantona and supplemented by a blend of top-class, experienced professionals and homegrown youngsters, Sir Alex Ferguson's team thrilled their way to success in both the Premier League and FA Cup just a year after suffering last-gasp heartbreak in both competitions.

There was no clue of what was to come when the season began with an opening day defeat at Aston Villa. So comprehensive was the loss for a side which had sold Paul Ince, Andrei Kanchelskis and Mark Hughes, that BBC pundit Alan Hansen was moved to remark: "You can't win anything with kids."

The kids certainly managed to make a fist of it, winning five of the next six Premier League games ahead of the return of Cantona, who had spent nine months on the sidelines after clashing with a Crystal Palace supporter at Selhurst Park. "The young lads had always been in awe of him," Gary Neville later reflected. "None of us got to know him well, but there was a vast, unspoken respect for him. We were desperate to impress him."

THE KING

'Back with a bang' is probably one of the best phrases to describe Eric Cantona's triumphant return to football after being banished to serve a nine-month suspension. The team's inspiration, the captain and the scorer of some of the season's most vital goals, Eric almost single-handedly drove the Reds on to Double glory. Seeing the Frenchman score the cup final winner in the dying seconds at Wembley was the kind of ending only a club like United could conspire to create.

THE KIDS

Famously written off on the first day of the season, the kids – namely David Beckham, Nicky Butt, Ryan Giggs, Gary Neville, Phil Neville and Paul Scholes – would go on to be the mainstay of the United team for many years and all played a vital role in the club's greatest ever achievement when a historic Treble was claimed in 1999.

Liverpool were the opposition as Cantona returned to action, and the Frenchman scored a second-half equaliser to secure a 2-2 draw for Ferguson's men and cap his comeback in style. Thereafter, the Reds' form was stop-start until the turn of the year, when the resumption of FA Cup duties and the need to make up a colossal 12-point deficit to league leaders Newcastle served to focus all minds.

Cantona scored the only goal of a hard-fought game at West Ham almost exactly a year after his Selhurst Park indiscretion, and the evening proved to be the watershed in United's season. He also demonstrated his growing restraint by playing the role of peacemaker as Hammers defender Julian Dicks and Reds striker Andy Cole threatened to come to blows after a flashpoint.

Before long, United's no.7 provided another invaluable contribution as he volleyed home the only goal of the game as the Reds, inspired by some goalkeeping heroics from Peter Schmeichel, staged a smash-and-grab win at Newcastle. Thereafter, the Magpies began dropping points at an astonishing rate, losing five of eight games, while Cantona and his colleagues won 13 of their last 15 league matches of the season.

Cantona's form was sensational, with an eight-game spell yielding seven goals which directly added nine points to the Reds' tally. The only shock came when he didn't score in the season finale at Middlesbrough, but mercifully David May, Cole and Ryan Giggs all did to secure the return of the Premier League title.

THE KEY GAMES

12 points behind leaders Newcastle United with only 10 games remaining – the Reds could have been forgiven for thinking that even a win at St James' Park would not have been enough to catch Kevin Keegan's men. Under Sir Alex Ferguson though, anything was possible and the Double dream became a reality. Cantona's volleyed winner on Tyneside set the ball rolling, with two more vital strikes, sealing victories at home to Arsenal, Spurs and Coventry, coming after a crucial late-leveller at QPR. A 3-0 win at Middlesbrough sealed the title, before Eric stepped forward once more against our arch-rivals at Wembley.

Fittingly, especially for a man who would go on to a career in acting after he retired from football, Eric ended the campaign in the spotlight. For the third straight season, the Reds made it to Wembley for the FA Cup final, this time against Liverpool, and a largely dire game was enlivened in the dying stages by Cantona's spectacular winner.

Almost 20 years have now elapsed since that joyous campaign, with Cantona due to celebrate his 50th birthday in May 2016, yet the passage of time will do nothing to dull the memories of an unforgettable campaign in which the King and the kids reigned supreme.

Foundation

LEGENDS ARE BACK!

CHARITY MATCH

14 JUNE 2015, OLD TRAFFORD

UNITED LEGENDS 4

(SAHA 9, YORKE 39, COLE 45, BLOMQVIST 83)

BAYERN MUNICH ALL-STARS 2

(ZICKLER 16, TARNAT 42)

BLAST FROM THE PAST

ALL-STAR CHARITY MATCH PROVIDES HUGE BOOST FOR MU FOUNDATION

United emerged victorious from the second instalment of a two-legged legends match with Bayern Munich in June 2015, raising over £700,000 for the Manchester United Foundation.

A 3-3 draw at the Allianz Arena in the summer of 2014 had left the tie intriguingly poised ahead of the second leg, and an entertaining 4-2 victory at Old Trafford gave the Reds a 7-5 aggregate success.

Fittingly, against the team beaten in May 1999 to secure an unprecedented Treble, Dwight Yorke, Andy Cole and Jesper Blomqvist – all members of the team that beat Bayern on that famous night – were on the scoresheet for the Reds, for whom Louis Saha opened the scoring.

Alexander Zickler and Michael Tarnat – two Bayern veterans from 1999 – reduced the arrears and kept the Old Trafford crowd entertained, but victory was seldom in doubt for a United side boasting nine Champions League winners in the starting XI.

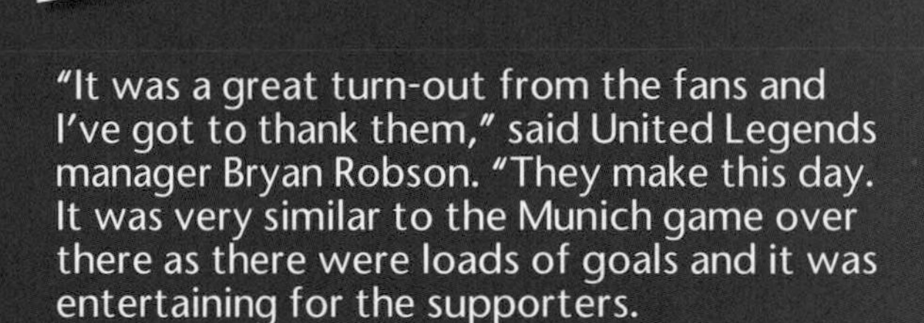

"It was a great turn-out from the fans and I've got to thank them," said United Legends manager Bryan Robson. "They make this day. It was very similar to the Munich game over there as there were loads of goals and it was entertaining for the supporters.

"Bayern are a top club. They do everything with a bit of class and are really friendly towards other clubs. A big thanks to them too as they brought such a big squad over and have given us a really good game. It's meant to be a family day out and that's what the fans got, with a few nice goals thrown in as well!"

While Robson and his side were able to savour victory over their Bayern counterparts, it was unquestionably the United Foundation who benefited most from a memorable afternoon.

Manchester United: Van der Sar (van der Gouw 61); P.Neville (Martin 77), Johnsen (Dublin 40), Stam, Irwin (Silvestre 40); Fortune (Blackmore 77), Park (Poborsky 46), Scholes (Thornley 77); Yorke (Beardsmore 77), Saha (Blomqvist 17), Cole (Ritchie 67).

Bayern Munich: Butt; Jorginho (Sternkopf 69), van Buyten, R.Kovac (Witeczek 46), Pflugler (Kreuzer 46); van Bommel (Gaudino 46), Breitner (Tarnat 20 (Rummenigge 61)), N. Kovac (Schupp 46 (Breitner 78)), Paulo Sergio; Zickler, Makaay (Zimmermann 69). Sub not used: Junghans

QUIZZES AND PUZZLES

SPOT THE DIFFERENCE

CAN YOU WORK OUT THE EIGHT DIFFERENCES BETWEEN THESE TWO PHOTOGRAPHS?

ANSWERS ON PAGE 60

WORDSEARCH

HIDDEN IN THE WORDSEARCH BELOW ARE THE NAMES OF 10 UNITED PLAYERS – CAN YOU FIND THEM?

A	R	E	R	R	E	H	J	O
E	I	A	A	R	R	O	M	S
K	D	N	A	E	N	A	D	H
C	E	R	I	E	T	N	N	A
I	E	G	S	A	I	I	S	W
R	S	M	A	L	L	I	N	G
R	O	A	B	T	I	L	I	B
A	E	S	I	H	P	M	E	M
C	E	Y	E	N	O	O	R	F

WORDS GO HORIZONTALLY, VERTICALLY, DIAGONALLY AND BACKWARDS.

ROONEY, JONES, SHAW, SMALLING, HERRERA

MEMPHIS, CARRICK, BLIND, MATA, FELLAINI

ANSWERS ON PAGE 60

GUESS THE GAME

WE'VE PICKED OUT 6 PHOTOS FROM SOME VERY FAMOUS UNITED MATCHES BUT CAN YOU ANSWER OUR QUESTIONS ABOUT EACH GAME?

GAME 1

Ashley Young celebrates a goal against Arsenal from August 2011 – how many goals did United score on the day?

GAME 2

This is one of Wayne Rooney's greatest strikes for the club and it sealed a 2-1 win over Manchester City, but who scored United's other goal in the match?

GAME 3

What game is this memorable photo from?

GAME 4

In what month and year did Ryan Giggs net a very famous goal against Arsenal?

GAME 5

Sir Alex bids farewell to the Reds after his final match in charge against West Brom at The Hawthorns in May 2013, but what was the final score?

GAME 6

This is the most famous night in United's history, but can you name the Reds' starting line-up for the 1999 Champions League final?

ANSWERS ON PAGE 60

TRUE OR FALSE?

A LOUIS VAN GAAL ONCE MANAGED REAL MADRID.

B MICHAEL CARRICK WON THE PREMIER LEAGUE TITLE IN HIS FIRST SEASON WITH UNITED.

C JUAN MATA SCORED HIS FIRST-EVER UNITED GOAL AGAINST ASTON VILLA.

D MEMPHIS JOINED UNITED FROM AJAX IN THE SUMMER OF 2015.

E THE FIRST TROPHY WAYNE ROONEY WON AS A UNITED PLAYER WAS THE LEAGUE CUP.

GUESS WHO?

IN EACH OF THESE PHOTOS WE'VE INCLUDED THE FEATURES OF THREE DIFFERENT UNITED STARS

PICTURE A

PICTURE B

PICTURE C

CAN YOU WORK OUT WHICH THREE PLAYERS MAKE UP EACH PICTURE?

ANSWERS ON PAGE 60

FIND FRED THE RED

CAN YOU SPOT FRED THE RED IN THIS PHOTO?

ANSWERS ON PAGE 60

QUIZ ANSWERS

SPOT THE DIFFERENCE, PAGE 54

WORDSEARCH, PAGE 55

A	R	E	R	R	E	H	J	O
E	I	A	A	R	R	O	M	S
K	D	N	A	E	N	A	D	H
C	E	R	I	E	T	N	N	A
I	E	G	S	A	I	I	S	W
R	S	M	A	L	L	I	N	G
R	O	A	B	T	I	L	I	B
A	E	S	I	H	P	M	E	M
C	E	Y	E	N	O	O	R	F

GUESS THE GAME, PAGE 56

Game 1, 8 goals – United won the game 8-2.
Game 2, Nani
Game 3, The 2008 Champions League final in Moscow when United beat Chelsea
Game 4, April 1999
Game 5, West Brom 5 United 5
Game 6, Schmeichel, G.Neville, Stam, Johnsen, Irwin, Beckham, Giggs, Butt, Blomqvist, Yorke, Cole.

TRUE OR FALSE? PAGE 58

A: False, van Gaal managed Barcelona, but not Real Madrid.
B: True, in 2006/07.
C: True, in March 2014.
D: False, he left PSV Eindhoven to join United.
E: True, in 2006.

GUESS WHO? PAGE 58

Pic A: Herrera's hair, Schneiderlin's eyes, Carrick's mouth
Pic B: Smalling's hair, Young's eyes, Memphis's mouth
Pic C: Shaw's hair, Januzaj's eyes, Mata's mouth

FIND FRED THE RED, PAGE 59

COMPETITION
WIN A SIGNED SHIRT

FANCY WINNING THE NEW UNITED SHIRT FOR THE 2015/16 SEASON, SIGNED BY SOME OF YOUR FAVOURITE PLAYERS?

THEN ANSWER THIS SIMPLE QUESTION.

RYAN GIGGS HAS PLAYED MORE GAMES FOR THE REDS THAN ANY OTHER PLAYER IN THE CLUB'S HISTORY - HOW MANY DID HE PLAY?

ENTER BY VISITING:

MANUTD.COM/ANNUAL2016

CLOSING DATE: MIDNIGHT ON 30 APRIL 2016.